BASIC TRAINING
FOR THE
WILDERNESS HUNTER

Preparing for Your Outdoor Adventure

MAURUS SORG, MD

Order this book online at www.trafford.com
or email orders@trafford.com

Most Trafford titles are also available at major online book retailers.

DISCLAIMER

The health fitness and training recommendations given in this book are for general
information only. Consult with your personal physician for the application of these
training principles to your training and preparation.

When preparing for an outdoors adventure, it is best that you ask your outfitter or
guide, if you have one, about training and preparation recommendations. If you
have a family physician or general internist who has personal knowledge, interest,
and competency in your outdoor plans, please consult with him or her and recognize
them for the tremendous asset that they are.

Printed in the United States of America.

ISBN: 978-1-4269-2882-6 (sc)

ISBN: 978-1-4269-4037-8 (e-book)

*Our mission is to efficiently provide the world's finest, most comprehensive
book publishing service, enabling every author to experience
success. To find out how to publish your book, your way, and have
it available worldwide, visit us online at www.trafford.com*

Trafford rev. 09/23/2010

 www.trafford.com

North America & international
toll-free: 1 888 232 4444 (USA & Canada)
phone: 250 383 6864 ♦ fax: 812 355 4082

Dedication: To Perry Klein

He was 42 years old and one of my very best friends. He was an NRA hunter safety instructor that instructed hundreds of students. He was in his prime, having recently lost 50 pounds at my suggestion, and in excellent physical condition.

We had recently survived a brutal Wyoming elk hunt. We joked that if we could survive this high altitude ordeal, we could survive anything. We planned to go into business together providing health recommendations to taxidermists and other sportsmen.

Several months later, I flew him over some ponds to check out the waterfowl. An hour later he was gone. As he swam the pond to retrieve his son's first harvest, he became tangled in a bed of weeds. He went under, never to come back up. It took three rescue teams to recover him.

We hunters, as outdoor adventurers, have special needs. If we do not pay attention to our environment, tragic events such as this can happen to us, even when we least expect it.

This book is in a way the result of me dealing with the tragic loss of my friend. It is also partially the result of my local hospital asking me to do a "Healthy Hunter Program" for the general public. I began to realize that there was plenty of information with regards to firearms safety, but there was an obvious lack of good information for hunters for health concerns and preparation for hunting.

Introduction

- -

- **It is no secret. I hate to see outdoors enthusiasts loose time and money!**

- -

It is also no secret that there are few reliable sources of information on the basics of how you begin to prepare yourself physically and mentally for an outdoors adventure.

I have been increasingly concerned about the hunting community, not only because it is aging, but also because of health and safety concerns. I have seen hunters who saved up many years for a "dream hunt of a lifetime" unable to complete it or suffer injury only because they were poorly prepared. I have also seen hunters ruin an expensive hunt for their companions for the same reason.

As a family and emergency medicine physician, I have repeatedly seen that simple things get the adventurer into trouble and that there are basic principles to any sporting endeavor. It is the simple things that will save you time and money, whether it is the everyday hunts or the outdoor "adventure hunt of a lifetime."

Five years ago a foot and ankle specialist told me that my

hunting days might be over because of an ankle fracture
and bad knees. I had recently dreamed of taking the
Grand Slam of North American sheep by backpack
hunting. As the specialist's words echoed in my brain, I
realized that it was time for a reality check.

I went to the Internet and tried to obtain high quality
information about the preparation for this type of
hunting. I got on as many forums as I could. I quickly
discovered that there was very little reliable information
for someone like me: an older hunter with injuries,
trying to do some of the most difficult hunting
imaginable. Some of the recommendations read like a
textbook in physical therapy. Other recommendations
were downright dangerous. Fortunately, I have a
background in sports medicine. By applying and using
simple training techniques, I was able to complete my
first backpack in the Northwest Territories. Since then I
have successfully completed four more backpack hunts,
two of them in the Unit 501 of Montana, arguably some
of the roughest terrain in the lower 48 states. Today I am
in better shape than I ever have been and my injuries
seem to be stable and actually improving.

Almost anyone can participate in activities as extreme
as a backpack sheep, elk, or goat hunt if they are willing
to take the time to prepare physically and mentally
and as long as they have the right equipment and
guidance. The principles are simple yet profound, and
not adhering to them will get you into trouble and waste
your precious time, money, and health.

Although there are excellent firearms safety courses
offered by the NRA and others and excellent bow
hunting educational classes offered by the national bow

hunting organizations, there is no formal course that I am aware of that exclusively deals with training issues, physical preparation, and general accident prevention specifically for the hunting community. This book is an attempt to bridge this gap to ensure that anyone who participates in this noble activity has at least some basic knowledge about preparation and safety for the various types of hunts that we do.

Hunting is my passion and I want to help as many others as I possibly can to safely and successfully enjoy this tradition. This simple book of no nonsense information should help you become the hunter that you should be... a "Wilderness Hunter." This book helps you make informed choices with regards to your preparation for that once in a lifetime hunt, extreme mountain hunt, or just simply keeping healthy and safe for all of your outdoor sports adventures.

Not all hunts are successful and not all hunting accidents are preventable due to the nature of our sport and unpredictable weather and geographic conditions. But we as hunters must make the utmost effort to keep our sport and ourselves safe and to make sure that the precious money that we have saved for the hunt is spent wisely.

At times the information in the book may seem oversimplified or too basic; however, the principles are timeless. This information belongs on the shelf of every outdoorsman or hunter as a basic reference for safety and preparation for whatever adventure that you choose to participate in.

Chapter One

- - - - - - - - - - - - - - - - - -

- **Who we are and what makes us want to hunt in the first place**
- **Why you are an outdoorsman**
- **Why now is so important**
- **Why you should congratulate yourself**
- **The characteristics of the WILDERNESS HUNTER**

- - - - - - - - - - - - - - - - - -

What is a WILDERNESS HUNTER?

A WILDERNESS HUNTER is an outdoor adventurer who hunts in areas remote from usual societal comforts and resources. Whether it is the sheep or elk hunter who enjoys mountainous terrain or the desert hunter on a self guided hunt....it is a hunter who has trained himself or herself to be self-sufficient and prepared for the worst that nature can throw at them. It is also a state of mind of preparedness, one that feels obliged to help others safely enjoy the adventure.

In the United States, participation in outdoors activities is at an all time low. As a nation we have become sedentary and "virtual" computer game dependent. We have become observers of life rather than participants.

We have lost the roots of our agrarian and adventurer hunter-gatherer past. As such we feel disconnected.

But not you! You are a hunter. As a WILDERNESS HUNTER you are the premier outdoors adventurer. You are able to participate in nature at a level that few others can imagine. You remain part of the life-death continuum that so many others have never experienced or have forgotten about. You recognize that without death there is no life. You participate in nature as its most basic level, traveling where there are no "established trails." You accumulate knowledge about the environment that few others can appreciate. You prepare yourself to face the worst situations knowing that you can prevail because you have physically and mentally prepared for them.

We as hunters should reframe our thinking and consider ourselves as OUTDOOR ADVENTURERS first and hunters second. If we can grasp that most of our preparation and training is geared towards the safety and preparation for our outdoor adventure and less so to the hunting techniques themselves, we will have already made a huge leap toward becoming the WILDERNESS HUNTER. Our genetic destiny is to be adventurer hunter-gatherers. Even the story of Jeremiah Johnson is more about overcoming obstacles than his hunting/trapping prowess.

We hunters also represent most of the meaningful financial contribution to the conservation of our precious wildlife resources. We do this through our participation in various foundations such as the Federation of North American Wild Sheep, Pheasants Forever, Ducks Unlimited, the Rocky Mountain Elk

Foundation, in addition to the purchase of game lands through license fees, land that many other non-hunters use.

We are our country's best-kept secret. While the anti-hunters constantly bash us, the National Sporting Goods Association most recent market report shows that hunting and firearms expenditures at $3.71 billion yearly is more than the $3.66 billion spent on golf equipment!

As a hunter, you have chosen an activity that can become a lifelong exercise habit. You have come to the realization that without exercise (movement) there is no life. And you have come to appreciate that many of societal woes come from uninterrupted work schedules AND LACK OF CONNECTION WITH OUR NATURAL ENVIRONMENT.

At least one State Department of Health has recognized the value of hunting as a health promotional activity. The Department of Health of South Dakota recognized that it had several programs for women, but nothing for men (I appreciate the number of women in the hunting sports, especially competition and archery). Since many men in South Dakota participate in hunting, they started the Healthy Hunter Series.

For many men, hunting as a cluster of related activities is their primary source of exercise. And each of us has our own reasons to and expectations of the hunt. How we hunt, who we hunt with, and how much we are willing to prepare all differ. You can start at any level to become the WILDERNESS HUNTER.

Walking is the safest of all activities and it is the

backbone of hunting. Although there are many hunting opportunities that involve the need for high levels of fitness, many do not. Whether it is scouting for sheds in the late winter, spring gobbler season, summer food plot development and game camera set up, or fall seasons, there is plenty to do to keep you fit all year around if you choose to do so. Regardless of the style of hunting that you choose, there is always a need to think like a WILDERNESS HUNTER.

Life long exercise habits together with good nutrition are the keys to longevity. Have you ever met an elderly person in decent shape that has not had at least a basic form of exercise? At the last Grand Slam Club/Ovis (GSCO) convention I met several sheep hunters in their eighties that looked 20 years their junior. They are fine examples of the WILDERNESS HUNTERS. As a family physician I have a theory that those that take time to enjoy life will also have more life to live.

There is time urgency for the hunter. You only have so many days to hunt. At some point in your life, even though you made the life long commitment to be a WILDERNESS HUNTER, you realize that you cannot climb the hills like you once were able to do. As Jack Atcheson, the famous sheep and big game outfitter, has trademarked "Hunt while you still can!" So you become like an airline pilot…you realize that you have to take care of yourself until you lose the privilege of participating in your passion.

One thing, however, is sure. We hunters have to raise the bar with regards to the public image of our sporting activities in order to save the sport and our unique connection with nature. This is what the process of becoming the WILDERNESS HUNTER is about! Without this effort we will fail to preserve our tradition and lose the battle for this noble heritage.

The characteristics of a WILDERNESS HUNTER

Why all of this fuss about being a WILDERNESS HUNTER? If you are going to participate in any sport–whether it is golf, bowling, or other–you most likely are trying to improve your scores and techniques. The $300 Calloway, the customized shoes, the expensive lessons by a "pro" are all considered standard fare.

We hunters, however, focus far too much of our time and resources on the equipment and less time on our skills. If you are like me, you would be a much more effective hunter preparing for the adventure and practicing our skills correctly with adequate equipment than by spending obscene amounts of cash on the latest, lightest, and tightest equipment. Too often we do not take the time to polish our skills and prepare ourselves before going on our hunting adventures. And we do not take the necessary time to prepare for adventures that could go awry.

BEING A WILDERNESS HUNTER IS TO ACKNOWLEDGE THE SERIOUSNESS OF OUR SPORT.

Any time that you engage the natural environment, there is always a chance you could end up dealing with the unexpected. You owe it to yourself, to your family, and to the sport to make the best effort you possibly can to keep this sport and yourself safe.

Why you need to prepare

The key quality that separates the WILDERNESS HUNTER from the rest of the pack is his or her commitment to preparation and excellence in the sport.

Every year many hunters waste precious dollars by being poorly prepared. They suffer countless numbers of needless injuries and even possibly death. Sometimes these are "hunts of the lifetime" that involve many dollars and much time.

In the course of my busy practice, I see many successful people who have spent their lifetimes building successful businesses and saving their money. The primary reason that many of them do it is because they want to hunt with whomever they want, whenever they want, for as long as they want. I tell these successful professionals that they deserve to enjoy what they have worked for but they are not going to get it for free! They are going to have to invest time and energy into preparation so that they have many extra years to enjoy the fruits of their labor.

The sad truth is, however, that if you are not in good physical condition or make an effort to prepare yourself to become the WILDERNESS HUNTER, most likely you will not get the full benefit of the experience. As is often the case, your adventure may turn into a nightmare or at the minimum a disappointment.

One of the biggest complaints of big game outfitters is that their clients come poorly prepared with regards to their physical conditioning, mental preparation, and excess body weight. Another common complaint is that the client overestimates their abilities and level of fitness. Also, they often do not inform the outfitter of their serious medical problems. All of these factors impair the outfitter's ability to provide their hunters with an optimal hunt.

Your ability to adapt to different environments depends upon your level of fitness. Your injury rate, especially with regards to the cardiac and musculoskeletal systems, is decreased with increasing levels of fitness. In other words, to keep your hunting safe, you must be fit. You must make a commitment to year round fitness. You get to choose at what level. But when you are preparing for your adventure, you need to step it up for 2-3 months, longer if you are older because it takes you longer to train. It takes time and effort to prepare. The human machine is quite resilient and often forgiving. Preparation is your best insurance policy.

The attributes of the WILDERNESS HUNTER

In order to be a WILDERNESS HUNTER, the following are the essential attributes and traits that you must CONTINUE TO DEVELOP. Hunting is a lot like golf... you can never get too good at it.

To become a WILDERNESS HUNTER you must:

- ☑ Be both heat and cold tolerant

- ☑ Be expert in heat and cold management and calorie management

- ☑ Be patient and almost trance like at times

☑ Have a cool head and have to be a good navigator

☑ Have adequate amounts of endurance and strength

☑ Be a rugged individualist while at the same time being a team player

☑ Have a sense of humor

☑ Be able to communicate with nature

☑ Love moisture, dampness, and cold

☑ Be a meteorologist, biologist, and geologist

☑ Be able to deal with high levels of frustration

☑ Be a strategist

☑ Have good vision and eyesight

☑ Be aware of your surroundings at all times

☑ Be as concerned with the health and safety of those you are hunting with as for yourself.

☑ Love children and puppy dogs (maybe not necessary, but it sure does help!)

Now that you know who a WILDERNESS HUNTER is, what your ideal characteristics should be, and why you should prepare, we are going to find out the differences in the types of hunting that we do.

Chapter Two

- **The types of hunts and how you must prepare as a WILDERNESS HUNTER to get the most for your time and money**
- **Why you must know the differences between the types of hunts**

Regardless of the type of hunting, your outdoor adventure as a WILDERNESS HUNTER should be fun and safe. We need to reduce the many types of hunts into simple elements and understandable categories. Once you understand the principles, you will be able to prepare for your hunt as a WILDERNESS HUNTER with a different outlook.

Safety and preparation are inseparable twins. Most accidental deaths are preventable and occur when the hunter is poorly prepared or uses bad judgment, takes unnecessary risks, show poor gun handling techniques, or uses bad tree stand tactics. Alcohol intoxication continues to take its toll especially when it comes to ATV use. If you just understand these facts, you will have made a significant improvement in your safety IQ.

Each sport has basic rules that you must understand or you are doomed to failure. As a WILDERNESS HUNTER you already intuitively know this.

Basic principles of what you must accept:

- Preparation and safety are an inseparable part of the hunt.

- It is usually the simple things that get you into trouble.

- Disasters usually are the result of a series of events, each of which by themselves appear insignificant but in combination lead to disaster. This, however, gives you multiple opportunities for intervention and prevention.

Types of hunts and why you must prepare as a

WILDERNESS HUNTER

He was 42 years old and one of my very best friends. He was an NRA hunter safety instructor that instructed many hundreds of students. He was in his prime, having recently lost 50 pounds of weight, and in excellent physical condition. We had recently survived a brutal Wyoming elk hunt. As he swam across a pond at dusk to retrieve his son's first Canadian goose, he was choked by hidden reeds. It took three rescue teams and two days to find and recover him.

Accidents like this are often not preventable. But most of them are with a little planning and foresight.

We, as outdoor adventurers and WILDERNESS HUNTERS, have special needs. If we do not pay attention to our environment, tragic events such as this can happen when we least expect it. A casual swim in a pond to retrieve a bird becomes an extreme situation in which there is no escape. This need for exceptional vigilance to our environment separates us from many participants in other sporting activities.

If you think that all hunting is just the same, you are missing golden opportunities to prepare and to prevent injuries. Although it sounds simple, in order to prepare yourself optimally you need to think of your hunting adventures as falling into three separate categories:

Casual hunts

Potentially extreme hunts

Extreme hunts

Casual hunts

Casual hunts are low risk hunts with mild to moderate physical effort and risk. Such hunts would include small game hunting and waterfowl hunting in warm weather like my friend. You might not think of this as a wilderness hunt. Usually this type of hunting requires a low level of conditioning and preparation. Just hop in your truck and go hunting. This is the easiest and probably the most common of the hunting situations and seldom involves significant injury. Firearms safety is still critical for this type of hunting.

Potentially extreme hunts

This category of hunts is the most dangerous, yet it gives you the most opportunity to prevent accidents.

Although this type of activity may require only mild
to moderate physical conditioning and may approach
what you might consider as wilderness hunting, there is
a potential for unpredictable occurrences that become
a high risk and/or involve high physical effort and
require a relatively high level of physical conditioning.
Examples include cold weather hunting where there is a
possibility of inclement weather and sudden exposure to
brutal weather, periods of intense physical activity, or the
potential for becoming "lost." Another example would
be group hunts where individual members who are less
than optimally prepared suddenly become "lost."

Extreme hunts

These types of hunts involve high risk and/or high
physical requirements and typically represent what
wilderness hunting is about. Usually the risks and
physical requirements are known and can be planned
in advance. Usually the participant recognizes the need
for intense physical fitness training and preparation.
Often this hunt has the need for special equipment like
ice picks, special boots, custom rifles, and backpacks.
Another important characteristic of the extreme hunt
is that rescue is often extremely difficult and untimely.
For this type of hunt, however, the hunter is usually well
prepared.

So why do I put so much emphasis on dividing
hunting into these separate categories? It is because
the potentially extreme hunt is usually where the
preventable injuries and death occur.

Take for instance bear hunting in Pennsylvania. For this
type of hunting you normally scramble to recruit 10-25

hunters of various ages and physical condition, throw
them all together for the first organized hunt of the
season, and start to drive the brush and side hills for the
elusive bruin. It goes without saying that you will almost
certainly have members in your hunting party that are
totally unfamiliar with the hunting territory, and other
new hunters who are doing this on an impulse and are
not well dressed or prepared.

In bear season the weather is already miserable, or it
will soon become miserable with that Pennsylvania scud
that you cannot call either rain or snow. Search and
rescue almost always gets called out somewhere and
usually finds a cold and wet hunter who in the best-case
scenario has found religion again and in the worst case
may be hypothermic and frostbit. Why there aren't more
fatalities, I don't understand.

The same thing can happen in deer season when a
hunter starts to follow a track and it begins to snow.
I can't tell you the number of times I have been
"temporarily disoriented" for a half-day or so. Snow
changes everything, and the landmarks disappear. If you
hunt in snow, you already know what I am talking about.
It doesn't take long in the deep woods of north central
Pennsylvania to become confused. You have worked up a
sweat, you are cold, you don't know where you are, and
nighttime is here. You better know what to do. You need
to think like a WILDERNESS HUNTER!

Archery has interesting challenges that make me put it
in this category. For the most part, archery is a sedentary
activity of sitting in tree stands for countless hours in
reasonable weather. You must be prepared, though,
because you need much upper body strength for proper

bow handling. The problem is that most bow hunters like height and 30 feet with a climbing stand is not out of the question. There is a science to tree stand safety, especially with tree climbing stands. There is too much temptation to cheat on the safety techniques to get into and out of tree stands safely and also to cheat on the restraint systems once you are in the stand.

Tree stand hunters are sometimes required to expend intense physical effort to deal with a compromising situation, usually as a result of carelessness. Examples include a hunter suspended by a restraint in a compromising position or one that has actually fallen and now must deal with a potentially fatal injury. You need to think like a WILDERNESS HUNTER.

The winter goose and duck hunter always recognizes the chance of hypothermia from a sudden dunk into a frozen lake. You better think like a WILDERNESS HUNTER, because it does not get much more extreme than that.

There are countless other examples of weather related hunting situations that have the potential to deteriorate to become wilderness events. Just recognizing the importance of this may encourage you to take the necessary precautions to plan ahead and maybe get yourself into a little better condition in order to survive the unpredictable.

With extreme hunts the risks are there, but usually the hunter has carefully weighed and prepared for them well in advance. Preparation is mandatory. The risks are there, but usually the necessary precautions have been

made. You are already thinking like a WILDERNESS
HUNTER.

In the next chapter we will talk about the basics
of preparation, but please keep this in mind: the
potentially extreme hunting situation is the one that you
should always prepare as if you were a WILDERNESS
HUNTER.

Chapter Three

- **Preparation will save you money...and possibly your hunt**

He was one of the nicest hunters that I ever met. He was a big fellow who appeared to be in reasonable shape. He was here at sheep camp with me because he won a sheep hunt at one of the more famous sheep drawings. He had a vast experience hunting elk in the northwest United States. His gun was a standard nine-pound elk rifle and he wore Woolrich clothes and heavy boots. Four days into the hunt he "had enough." He was exhausted both physically and mentally.

He passed on the opportunity to finish his seven-day dream hunt in some of the most pristine and productive Dall sheep country in the world. He admittedly was not a WILDERNESS HUNTER.

You may have heard the statement that "life is about the journey and not the destination." In my opinion, the same should be said for hunting. Preparation is as important as the actual physical act of hunting. With some types of extreme hunts, as many as two out of seven hunters fail because of the lack of physical and mental preparation. This is a tragic waste of money with the cost of guided sheep and elk/mule deer hunts being what they are today.

Guides and outfitters all tell the same story. Most of them say that only one third of their hunters come optimally prepared. Often they are in poor physical condition and have unrealistically high expectations of the hunt. They frequently overestimate their physical prowess and often have serious medical conditions, which, of course, they do not inform the guide or outfitter about. Let me give you some examples:

- The 400-pound fellow that told his outfitter on the phone that he jogged three miles daily (true story!)

- The pale, sweaty, and nauseated elk hunter whose wife tells him at 10,000 feet altitude in front of his guide, "See, honey, I told you that your doctor said that your heart won't be able to take this trip because of your heart attack two weeks ago!" (another true story!)

- The elk/mule deer outfitter who confided in me that he "upgraded" his horses to draft stock because his hunters are getting too large.

Sometimes, but not often, it can be the other way around. Most guides are reasonably trained and responsible. One problem that I have seen several times, though, is the guide with a drug or alcohol problem. This is probably uncommon, but you need to be aware of it. You must recognize the problem for what it is to "negotiate" a better effort from the guide.

I once hunted with a guide that had a drug problem. I know of a guide who wears an insulin pump and another that has anaphylactic reactions to beestings. These are all good things for the hunter to know, especially if the hunter has a background in a health related field. As I will explain in a later chapter, I often carry emergency supplies in case the guide gets ill. The guide is my ticket to a successful hunt and I do not want to jeopardize that!

Taking the time to physically prepare yourself and to become a WILDERNESS HUNTER dramatically improves your odds of success. Imagine these scenarios:

The hunter comes into camp. The guide sizes him up to see if he can "break him." Now not all guides do this, but some do. They figure if they can "break" the hunter they can quit the hunt early, get back to camp, and maybe get some drinks. I swear some guides do it just for the pleasure of inflicting pain! Your job as a WILDERNESS HUNTER is not to let your guide "break you." You need to be in decent shape just so he or she cannot do this to you. If he or she can't, you may get a decent hunt out of them.

Much more often, however, there are responsible guides who see you are an extra effort fellow or gal (i.e. a WILDERNESS HUNTER). Those guides sometimes will take you to the more pristine and more difficult places to access because they know that you are up to the challenge and won't complain.

Your ability to adapt to different environments depends upon your level of conditioning. The more physically fit you are the more easily you adapt, and more importantly, the less likely you are to become injured. This is especially true with regards to the cardiac and musculoskeletal systems.

Most of us make the mistake of accumulating equipment instead of skills. We buy the best boots but do not properly break them in. We buy a custom rifle but do not shoot it enough to become competent. It is far better to use what you have, as long as it is adequate, and then practice the daylights out of it. Familiarity breeds competency.

The same applies to physical and mental preparation. You do not need expensive equipment to get into shape or prepare for the emergency. You just need to practice with what you have. Everything that you truly need to get into great shape costs little to nothing (although some equipment may be more efficient for your training).

Preparing for the hunt and becoming a WILDERNESS HUNTER is hard work, but it should be fun. Preparation is your best insurance policy as a hunter. And the amount of preparation that you needs varies with the type of hunting that you do, with extreme hunting demanding the highest duration of training and the highest level of commitment.

The three inescapable principles of physical training and hunt

Before you can commit to WILDERNESS HUNTING you need to accept three inescapable truths. The violation of any of them is a fatal event.

The phenomenon of the least common denominator

Murphy's Law

The McGyver principle

Everyone has experienced the phenomenon of the least common denominator. This principle states that the chain is only as strong as its weakest link. The fellow that is the most out of shape or in poor health will absolutely ruin the hunt. The person with the weakest navigation skills will get lost on the easiest drive. The lamest horse will determine the speed of the pack.

Murphy's Law is self-explanatory. If there is the remotest possibility of something happening, especially if it is critical, it will happen. If you are not prepared for rain, it will rain. The further you are from an easy rescue, the more likely you will become lost. That piece of equipment that you thought you wouldn't need you now need. You get the picture.

The McGyver principle is the holy grail of WILDERNESS HUNTING. Duct tape, safety pins, and garbage bags can be turned into anything. It is guaranteed by Murphy's Law that you will not have all of the necessary equipment, so you have to learn to improvise.

Why is it so important to recognize these three principles? If you can recognize these three laws and use them as guidelines to plan and prepare your hunt, they become very useful to you in pointing out potential flaws in your planning. For instance, you may want to take a closer look at your hunting roster and rethink your hunting strategy, or at least rearrange hunters to honor the law of the least common denominator. Or you, the WILDERNESS HUNTER, may not ask certain individuals to join you on certain hunts because they just are not up to the challenge.

Using the application of Murphy's Law, you begin to

think and prepare for the most unlikely events. Yes, it is
extra effort, but the failure to apply this principle will
eventually cause you a serious cash crisis or a ruined
hunt.

The McGyver principle is critical for your self-
confidence. Making do with what you have gives you
great confidence, and in high stress and panic situations,
you need all of the confidence that you can muster. The
application of this principle takes a little homework. You
need to study the different uses of basic equipment and
tools. This can be quite fun, however, as your confidence
grows and you realize that most of what you really need
to survive is close at hand! The thorough familiarization
with this principle is like an extra insurance policy for
you to insure your safety and survivability.

Other principles and guidelines for the WILDERNESS
HUNTER include:

Heart health takes precedence over all types
of preparation because of the threat of sudden
incapacitation and death. The function of the heart is to
feed your legs, and your training program should reflect
this.

The more extreme the hunt the longer and harder you
must prepare for it. This is especially true the older you
get. And if you are a woman, you might have to train
longer and harder for endurance because many sports
specialists feel that women cannot gain endurance as
quickly as men.

If your anticipated hunting is extreme or involves cold
weather, you should seriously think about avoiding

calorie restricted diets close to the time of the hunting activity. You simply do not want to be in a calorie-depleted state when you face the challenges of cold weather outdoor sports. You will be able to stay warmer, and if you are unfortunate enough to get into one of those survival situations, that extra reserve that you have may come in handy. (Of course, do not go overboard... a little jiggle is OK.)

When it comes to high altitude hunting, you must pay much closer attention to breathing issues. Some of the most serious outdoor emergencies occur at altitude. Minimizing the risk of altitude will serve you well as a WILDERNESS HUNTER.

In summary, in order to be a WILDERNESS HUNTER you absolutely must pay attention to these principles. Please let your hunting companions (or guide) know of your health problems and how to deal with them. Be truthful and honest about your exercise capacities, and your outfitter will do everything in his or her power to give you the hunt that best matches your abilities.

Now that you have a grasp of the basic principles, we will further discuss preparation for your outdoor adventure. We will start with the principles of individual sport training and then move onto physical fitness and health, clothing, personal communication and navigation, first aid, survival equipment, and mental preparation.

Chapter Four

- **The principles of individual sport training: mountain sheep butt heads and eat grass...you need a better training program**

Another one of the guiding principles for the WILDERNESS HUNTER is that you must take personal responsibility for your individual training. This chapter will guide you through the process, first with basic principles and then with some training recommendations.

The health and fitness industry is fickle. In the 10 years that I operated my health and fitness club, I saw many fitness fads come and go. Every year there are new fitness gurus, new dietary programs, and new ways to train for the ultimate physique. There are low carbohydrate diets, low fat diets, high fat diets, raw diets, and biblical diets. You get the picture. Today's truths are tomorrow's fallacies. That being said, there are timeless truths with regards to physical conditioning and diet advice that will forever stand the test of time.

Few accurate articles have been written about the best way to train for the extreme hunting adventure and to prepare you to become a WILDERNESS HUNTER. Before I did my first sheep hunt, I researched on

how to go about training myself for this adventure.
I went to Grand Slam Ovis, and Dennis Campbell
sent me an article about the "Six Minute Hill" which
involves climbing a hill for about six minutes, coming
back down, and doing pushups. Other websites like
24HourCampfire.com and Kifaru.com had additional
information through their forums. Tony Russ's "Sheep
Hunting in Alaska" was very useful. Other than this,
there was little useful information.

Many of the books, which were written for the
mountaineering and hiking community, gave detailed
information about strengthening and training
programs. They were too complicate and reminded me
of textbooks in physical therapy and sports medicine. I
just don't have time to learn a complicated routine or
work 20-30 exercises and stretches into my routine.

For any exercise program to be successful, especially
for the WILDERNESS HUNTER, it has to be easy
to follow and very efficient. It also has to follow the
principles of individual sport training.

THE MOST IMPORTANT PRINCIPLES OF INDIVIDUAL SPORT TRAINING

Almost all of effective sport training and exercise programs must incorporate these five principles:

The KIS (Keep It Simple) Principle

The Principle of Proximity

The Pareto Principle (Leverage)

The Perfection Principle

The Law of Diminishing Return

As stated in the introduction to the chapter above, the KIS (Keep It Simple) Principle is probably the most important. The simpler the routine is the more likely that you will follow it. You can keep your training shorter and less complicated.

The Principle of Proximity states that the closer you are to your project, the more likely you are to do it. Take for instance the dream of mine to build an airplane. All of the people who have successfully completed their projects tell me that it was only when the project was close at hand (e.g., garage, basement) were they able to complete it. The same principle applies to exercise program and equipment. For most of us, the ideal place for our exercise routine to become a WILDERNESS HUNTER should be in the home or near work. There are those that need a gym and have the time to do so. That isn't most of us. The gym doesn't have the equipment I like anyway.

Whenever you are designing an exercise routine, you want to get the biggest bang for the buck. This is where the Pareto Principle comes in. Pareto was an Italian economist who recognized that 80% of the value in a project was found in 20% of the work. This principle applies to nearly everything, including an exercise program for the WILDERNESS HUNTER. You must design an exercise program that will give you 80% of what you need in 20% of the time. It also forces you to recognize that only 20% of the exercises that you presently are doing are giving you 80% of your results!

For the time challenged individual, this is great news. It allows you to focus on the most important exercises while avoiding or minimizing the lesser important ones. Yeah! Fewer exercises!

The Perfection Principle and its cousin the Law of Diminishing Return are the two other principles that are necessary to design a program of individual sport training. The Perfection Principle states that it takes as much work to go from 95th percentile of perfection to the 99th percentile as it does to go from 0 percentile to the 95th percentile. The Law of Diminishing Return states that there comes a certain point where increased effort will result in decreasing benefits.

Scientific study validates the Perfection Principle. Study after study shows that you get the most benefit when you take a sedentary individual and make them mildly fit as opposed to taking a moderately fit individual and making them highly fit. Conversely, there appears to be a point where more exercise becomes harmful to you. For runners it is some point between 30-40 miles a week. Beyond this your immune system is slowly torn apart and your chance of injury and illness dramatically increases.

This is great news! You do not need to be an extreme athlete to be an effective WILDERNESS HUNTER. You only need to get to a certain point in your training, and beyond that point your efforts to improve your level of fitness are going to be relatively wasted. As is true for most situations, the 95th percentile is plenty good enough unless you want to be a competitive athlete or other gold medal winner. You will be able to recognize your 95th percentile. Forget the marathon; let's go on a long climb!

If you can incorporate these five principles into your exercise training, you already know more than most athletes. Now for the real work!

Fitness

Every WILDERNESS HUNTER must understand the concept of FITNESS. Everyone has their own idea of what fitness or being fit means. There is a science to this.

Most sports medicine specialists agree that there are five components to fitness. These include:

Flexibility – your ability to move your muscles and joints through their range of motion

Muscular strength – how much force your muscles can generate

Cardiorespiratory endurance – how long and at what level of intensity that your heart and lungs can deliver oxygen to your tissues and remove waste and maintain your musculoskeletal system

Muscular endurance – how long your muscles can maintain repeated contractions

Body composition – the ratio of lean body mass to fat

As a **WILDERNESS HUNTER,** you should train primarily for cardiorespratory and muscular endurance, with less emphasis on muscular strength, flexibility, and body composition (unless you are an archer that needs a minimum of upper body strength to pull the bow). In order to accomplish this, you need to recognize your own cardiorespiratory and muscular weaknesses and take the proper action to address them. In medicine we call this "empowering the patient." You must take personal responsibility for your own training program because your needs are different from others.

Hunters, in general, have to be common sense individuals because the unique pursuit of game animals demands this. You always have to be adapting to the environment and adjusting your strategy based on the actions of the quarry. This represents a central dilemma of the sport... YOU NEVER KNOW WHAT YOU ARE GETTING INTO.

This is especially true for the WILDERNESS HUNTER. The one thing that we know for sure is that when the hunt deteriorates you most likely are going to require a much higher level of fitness and you are going to need your skills as a WILDERNESS HUNTER. And most importantly, your physical condition has a lot to do with how quickly you adapt to changing environments.

If you apply the above principles, the exercises that you need to design your own sport-training program may or may not become obvious to you. Here are some suggestions:

Generally, the best way to train for an activity is to do the activity required in progressive degrees of difficulty while at the same time cross training enough to avoid injury. Always start slow and work up. Most sports injuries occur by doing too much too soon.

Your legs are your most important weapon as an adventurer/hunter. You must work to train and preserve them. It also helps to think that the primary duty of your heart and lungs are to support the activity of your legs.

It would be hard to imagine training for a mountain backpack hunt without actually doing backpacking. The same could be said for mountain hunting or horseback hunts. Focus on the core activity and try to duplicate it in your exercise routine. Design a program that you can increase progressively, like adding more weight to your backpack or climbing steeper hills. Try to incorporate the equipment that you are going to be using into your exercise routine. For instance, wear your backpack when you are on the stair climber. Use your walking poles for your downhill work.

The harder the hunt, the more you have to train and the mentally tougher you have to be. Nobody can train you to be mentally tough, but prolonged endurance exercise comes close. You have to experience discomfort for a prolonged period of time in order to become hardened. For me it is the prolonged backpack hikes that I do just before the hunt. You have to be in good shape before you attempt this though, or you may become quite discouraged. Once again, start slow and build up your tolerance.

Sometimes the best way to train is to ask the outfitter or guide what he or she would recommend. If the outfitter has been in business long enough, they have seen the end result of different training programs. They may have some valuable suggestions for you not only with regards to training but also for the types of equipment that you need.

Being consistent with the Pareto Principle, I believe that the optimal number of training exercises in any group is three. You should focus on three types of endurance exercises, three types of cross training sports, three types of stretching exercises, and three types of strengthening exercises. This is not to say that you cannot do more. You can do as many as you want, but 80% of the value in your training is going to come from the three core exercises in whatever focus you have. Professional athletes have to do much more because they have to strive for absolute perfection. You do not!

The following are examples of how to use this principle of three exercises per group. Backpacking with moderately heavy loads, mountain biking, and cross-country skiing may represent adequate cross training for endurance. Pushups, pull-ups, and abdominal crunches may be all that you need for strength training. Matt Furey, the Internet exercise guru, recommends Hindu squats, Hindu pushups, and bridging exercises as the basic core for his Combat Conditioning.

Pick something that works for you. Your training program should enhance and protect your physical assets. You should choose your hunting style based on your physical capacity. Most training programs focus on endurance types of cardiovascular training with less importance on strength and flexibility (women cannot gain endurance as quickly as men). You need to know what your weaknesses are so that you can deal with them. If you do not feel comfortable doing this for yourself, find a trainer or someone else qualified in the health or fitness industry, or contact us at OUTDOOR SPORTS MEDICINE for a consultation. And remember to cross train to avoid injury.

Choosing exercise equipment deserves a whole book. You do not, however, need a gym. Bleachers and stairs are good. Everything that you truly need is within your reach and costs virtually nothing. Good equipment is adequate and costs are deceiving.

If you insist on equipment, however, here are some of my recommendations:

With regards to sheep and other types of mountain hunting, the Stairmaster is standard fare. Better yet, in my estimation, is the Stairmaster PT7000 stepper mill, which is like moving stairs. If you can find one, you may find that it is the ticket. The Versaclimber is an excellent way to build up endurance especially with the upper body. I have worked out on the Bowflex Treadclimber, and I have found it to be excellent. Other WILDERNESS HUNTERS like treadmills and exercise bikes. I find them boring. A 2x4 on a floor makes an excellent balance beam. Any kind of weight bench with free weights is adequate if you plan on using it. A pull up bar is inexpensive.

Whichever pieces of equipment or training regimen that you use, please choose something that you enjoy. If you do not enjoy it, you will quit.

With regards to the extreme and potentially extreme hunts, I cannot overemphasize the need for endurance training. You can only do this by working up a sweat for a prolonged period of time (more than one hour). I am convinced that the reason the our society is obese and experiences increasing incidence of conditions such as diabetes not only relates to the commercialization of a poor quality diet (albeit with a long shelf life) but also to the fact that most of us are endurance exercise starved.

Besides your legs and heart, your feet are the most important area of the body for the hunter. Good boots that are properly broken in are no guarantee that you will not have problems with your feet. There are simple things that you can do to help aching feet. Perhaps the best experts on this subject are runners. They are constantly "tuning" their running shoes. The take home message for the WILDERNESS HUNTER is that you can make small adjustments that make large differences in your performance.

An insert such as an arch support or heel lift is easy to implement. Or simply pieces of moleskin glued into your shoes will do the trick. You need to do this yourself because none of us are perfectly symmetrical. There can be as much as a full shoe size difference between your right and left foot. One foot may have a higher arch or be slightly wider. Experimenting with the inserts may solve the most complicated of problems.

You may or may not need ankle support. I do because of a previous ankle fracture. There usually is a price to be paid for ankle support and that is a heavier boot. Try several boots to see what your needs are.

The same can be said for knee braces. Sometimes simple wraps or elastic knee braces make large differences, but oftentimes they do not. You have to experiment for yourself to find out.

With regards to shoulders and hips, they usually take care of themselves. If you are having problems with these joints, you might as well see a health professional that can accurately diagnose and treat your condition, as these tend to be complicated structures.

Back health is extremely important to the WILDERNESS HUNTER. More hunters than not have back trouble. There are no easy explanations for this except that a strong flexible back is usually healthier than a weak stiff back. Most people forget that the abdomen and its musculature is the front part of the back.

There is a whole field in exercise physiology called "core training" that devotes itself to strengthening the body's core (trunk/back). If you are interested in this type of training, there are many programs to help you do so. My core-strengthening program is to throw on a backpack

and do hills. But what works for me may not work
for you. And if you have back trouble, please consult
the health professional that you have the greatest
confidence in.

You would be well served to remember that the human
body is a biomechanical unit. You have to try to balance
all of your training activities so that you do not overstress
any separate part of the unit. That knee pain you may be
experiencing just may be coming from the hip. And that
weakness in your legs may be coming from your neck.
Once again, if you cannot figure out why something is
hurting, please consult a health care professional.

As you get older you realize that you have to make an
extra effort to preserve what you already have. In my
case I had to be sure that whatever training program I
was doing did not worsen my ankle injury or knees. In
your case it may be a bad back. An injury may set back
your training for weeks or months, but sometimes you
do not have months. Save what you have before you try
to improve it.

There are health hazards associated with inappropriate
or excessive training. When you hurt after a long
workout, some of it may be good and some bad. It is not
uncommon for muscles to ache after a workout. This
may not necessarily be bad, and sometimes the delayed
onset of muscle soreness can be prevented by Vitamin
E. Sore tendons and ligaments, however, are another
issue altogether. This soreness represents actual injury to
these structures. If you do not take the time to let them
heal, they could go on to rupture or tear.

No discussion about training should fail to include the

general principles of good health. The principles of living a long and healthy life are well known and should be followed. Here are some of the most useful:

- ☑ Stay involved in life. Wherever you are, be there. Live every day to the fullest.

- ☑ Get enough sleep. Usually this means about eight hours daily.

- ☑ Eat three meals daily of high quality food. This means more fruits and vegetables and less of everything else.

- ☑ Stay away from the three white poisons: white salt, white flour, and white sugar.

- ☑ Control your weight. Keep your BMI under 22 if at all possible. Yes, it is possible to be fit and fat, but it increases your risk of diabetes and hypertension.

- ☑ Use alcohol gingerly or not at all: a maximum of 2 drinks daily for men, one for women. A drink is defined as what would be commonly accepted as a single drink.

- ☑ Do not smoke.

- ☑ Do not abuse drugs and medications.

- ☑ Get medical help to optimize your genetic destiny.

- ☑ Practice good safety habits (USPHS guidelines)

There is a lack of information as to the optimal health screening criteria for the WILDERNESS HUNTER. Until we develop these criteria, we have to rely on standard recommendations. You need to have a good rapport with your personal physician and trust that he or she has an understanding of the physical requirements of your hunting situation. The following are the current recommendations with regards to stress tests and physical exams.

Physical exam and stress test

Starting at age 40 you should have a complete physical exam every 2-3 years. After the age of 50 you should have a yearly physical exam. Recommendations for stress tests vary, but if you want to be a WILDERNESS HUNTER and you are over the age of 40 and have two or more risk factors (high blood pressure, elevated cholesterol, diabetes, strong family history of heart disease, obesity, markedly sedentary lifestyle, or are known to have coronary artery disease), you need a stress test or another similar test to exclude coronary artery disease. Please understand, no screening or diagnostic test is perfect. Please consult your personal physician.

Once again, you need to have a good rapport with your personal physician. Make sure that he or she has a thorough understanding of the physical requirements of your hunting situation.

Now that you have a basic understanding of individual sport training for the WILDERNESS HUNTER, the next chapter will discuss individual topics with regards

to the essentials of preparation for any hunting
situation.

Chapter Five

- **Survival...your life depends upon it. It sounds sexy but it is the most serious part about hunting**

Every year you read stories about amazing survivals: someone who was in the snowy mountains for a week, in a boat without food or water for days to weeks, survivors of plane crashes. Then you read about tragic but preventable deaths where the individuals made poor decisions that cost them their lives. You have to feel a sense of sadness when reading these stories. Many of them could have been easily prevented.

There have been libraries of books and manuals written about survival. I have taken survival courses and have read several field manuals. My favorite reference, however, is Wilderness Medicine by Dr. Paul Auerbach. The Wilderness Medical Society has much high quality information available for the wilderness adventurer. Most of their information is geared to the health care professional or rescuer. In their chapter on survival, the following is what they have to say are the most important survival habits:

Critical survival skills

☑ The ability to swim well

☑ Expertise in the use of a map and a compass

☑ The ability to build a fire under adverse conditions

☑ A working knowledge of local weather patterns

☑ Familiarity with the special medical problems of the wilderness involved

☑ A survival kit appropriate for the topography, climate, and season

☑ Ability to construct appropriate types of survival shelters

☑ A working knowledge of natural hazards and how to predict and protect yourself from them and to avoid them

☑ Reading and analyzing accounts of survival stories

☑ Awareness of the psychological aspects of the survival situation and of the errors of judgment that can lead to a survival emergency

☑ Knowledge of edible plants and animals and basic hunting, fishing, and trapping

☑ Awareness that you should not travel into the wilderness alone and should always let others know of your destiny and time of return

One of the most important memory tricks that I have learned for survival is "WDW" which stands for WARM, DRY, WATER. When faced with a survival situation, it is always the highest priority to stay warm first, because if you develop hypothermia (low body temperature) your thinking will become clouded and you may make poor decisions. The next important decision is to stay dry because if you don't you will not be able to stay warm. Once you have the WARM and DRY under control, you should try to find a source of WATER. If you do these three things first you will most likely survive.

The approach to the survival situation is much like a game, a very serious game for the WILDERNESS HUNTER. There are rules that you must follow, but there are golden opportunities for you to use the skills and creativity that you have so religiously trained for.

A large part of the survival of any situation is communication. This begins by letting someone know where you are going and what time you will be back. One sheep hunter shared with me that when he is hunting sheep in Asia or elsewhere, the satellite phone is his most important piece of survival equipment. Fortunately with today's technology, the risks of traveling in the wilderness are becoming much less so.

Recently there has been a boon in personal ELTs. These have been made famous by the recent spectacular rescue on Mount Hood. These are electronic tracking devices that can pinpoint your location with amazing precision. You can send a signal for help. You just have to be sure that you do not push the wrong button. If you are going to be in a remote region for any length of time, I believe that at least one person in your party should have one. Your family can even track you from home to plot and follow your route.

Another piece of equipment that has revolutionized wilderness rescue is the cell phone, when service is available. They frequently work when nothing else will and can give medical help a heads up in what is coming and how to prepare. Remember, texting extends their range.

That being said, the most important communications device is your brain. Your brain is also your most important survival tool. Smoke, noise, and signal fires still work. A signal mirror and a whistle are still highly effective communication devices. If you can, always carry a portable radio. They have saved countless hunters from becoming lost. I often monitor different frequencies to make sure there is no one in distress.

Other sheep hunters have shared with me that the next most important survival tool especially when hunting remote areas overseas is the purchase of emergency medical evacuation insurance. This purchase must not be taken lightly as I will explain in the chapter on international hunting. These services are not all created the same.

Always have an escape plan. Wherever you are, be there. Be aware and pay constant attention to your surroundings so that you can recognize landmarks and plan your retreat. Constantly watch the weather. Maybe that is the pilot in me, but the weather can change in an instant and totally change the landscape, causing you to lose your bearings.

When reviewing the literature about survival, one common denominator always comes up. Those individuals that have the best chance of surviving have made it a habit to study survival. They have read stories about survival and the survivors. Perhaps it gives them hope and resolve. Whatever it gives them, you owe it to yourself to read accounts about survival in preparation for any adventure that may put you in harm's way.

Survival Equipment

The equipment that you choose often can mean the difference between a comfortable unexpected stay in the wilderness or a possible life threatening one. Once again, and I cannot say it enough, your brain is the most important survival tool.

It is interesting how some individuals can survive even if they are poorly prepared. I call this the "you got to be strong if you are going to be stupid syndrome." Wrecking your snowmobile or ATV and having to stay out all night in bitter cold with just a thin jacket or spending the night in the White Mountains of Vermont unprepared for the sudden changes in weather that occurs during your day hike are typical examples. Some people are strong enough to survive adverse conditions poorly prepared, but most of us are not.

The ideal characteristics of survival equipment for the WILDERNESS HUNTER are that they are always with you, weigh little, are carried unnoticed, and are totally adequate for your survival needs. Many commercial kits are available through sports stores like Dick's and, if you are not on an extreme hunt, may be quite adequate. There is, however, an unfortunate inverse relationship between the degree of difficulty of your hunt and the size of the survival kit that you can carry. Because of this, it is often best that you make your own.

In order for your equipment to be effective, it should be on you or immediately retrievable. Lanyards, belt pockets, game pouches, and vests are some examples. As far as equipment goes, at a minimum you must have a fire starter of some sort. In cold and damp weather, a fire may be the most important factor in your survival. A compass and signal equipment comes next.

Construction garbage bags, space blankets, safety pins, duct tape, and parachute cord are all useful. An extra water bottle or plastic bag that can be used to collect and to carry water is ideal.

Always consider brightly colored equipment, including your glasses. Get a can of fluorescent paint and mark some of your essential tools like your knife so that you do not misplace it when you need it the most. It can also save you from injury because you see where you have placed your sharp equipment such as your knife. My guide in British Columbia almost lost his glasses in the marshy growth and to solve that problem he tied a small piece of flagging tape to them. You might want to consider doing this to some of your other equipment like your high priced binoculars, especially if they are black or green.

Your survival kit needs to be adapted to each hunt. Do not just put a kit together and forget about it. Especially for the extreme hunt, you must familiarize yourself with the requirements of the hunt. Just as important, you have to familiarize yourself with the contents of your kit. It is estimated that 70% of hunters do not know how to use their emergency medical kit, including the epinephrine pen.

Practice a survival night when conditions are favorable and continue to hone your fire starting skills whenever possible. Invest in a light bivy sack for that unexpected night out. They cost about $25, weigh next to nothing, and are outstanding insurance.

Always carry a backup flashlight/headlamp. With the new generation of LED lights, there is no excuse for not doing this. The new LED lights that fit on or are built into the bill of the cap are a good backup, but you really should have a high quality headlamp. Other backup lighting like zipper lights work in a pinch. Some even have a compass on them, weigh nothing, and cost next to nothing.

There are many books on survival that you might want to read, but knowing how to survive is not enough to prepare your self for that ultimate hunting adventure. Follow along so that we can work you through the additional skills and knowledge that you need to successful complete your outdoors adventure as a WILDERNESS HUNTER.

Chapter Six

- **Weather related hunting injuries...do not let them ruin your hunt**

The rescue team was becoming exhausted. The missing hunter had traveled all night through the bitterly cold snowy forest. The lead tracker suddenly found a glove. Shortly later he found a hat. Several hundred yards later there was a coat. Unfortunately by the time they found the hunter he had died of exposure and hypothermia, but he was only wearing a minimum of clothes.

Of all the potential things that can cost you your life in a survival situation, weather related injuries rank at the top. Although heat related conditions cause their share of injuries, it is the cold related injuries that cause most of the injuries to the big game hunter. And the king of all cold related injuries is hypothermia.

Hypothermia (low body temperature) is common. Although we think of hypothermia on the bitterly cold days of mid winter, hypothermia surprisingly occurs most commonly in wet conditions between 50-70°F! The chief danger with hypothermia is that impairs your ability to think at a time when your ability to think clearly is critical.

The story at the beginning of the chapter demonstrates that a state of confusion with hypothermia is not that unusual. Hypothermia progresses from chills to confusion to lethargy. During the confusional stage, the person may feel paradoxically warm and begin to remove clothes at a time when the exact opposite is required for survival.

Another peculiarly dangerous fact about hypothermia is that it may occur slowly, almost unnoticed. I remember the heated discussion with a tall thin guide (8% body fat) that I had in a blinding snowstorm at 11,500 feet altitude. I was profusely sweating and desperately needed a rest and fluid after climbing 2500 feet. I was dressed warmly; he was not. I noticed that he was getting slightly confused and argumentative. He was starting to suffer from hypothermia at a time when I was beginning to suffer from heat exhaustion!

Although I desperately needed the rest, I plunged on and vowed never to do another sheep hunt again. But I recognized the subtle signs of hypothermia that he had, and I knew that there was no sense in arguing with him. I needed him to get back to camp. We managed to drop altitude and find camp. Sure enough, he had a moderate case of frostnip of his fingers that lasted the rest of his hunt, a tell tale sign that he had been too cold despite all precautions.

Risk factors for hypothermia include inadequate clothing, poor physical conditioning, dehydration, alcohol, exhaustion, and low body fat. The treatment is to warm up as quickly as you can by using whatever means you have.

Wilderness rescue teams are taught the mantra that anyone who is lost has hypothermia, dehydration, and hypoglycemia (low blood sugar) until proven otherwise. That is why it is always prudent for you as a WILDERNESS HUNTER to carry some source of calories and an extra water bottle on you at all times if water is not immediately available. Do this not only for yourself, but also for a fellow hunter that you may happen to come upon. I almost always carry a pint thermos of a hot beverage on cooler days to take off the chill and to have as backup in case I happen upon a lost hunter.

There are other cold induced injuries. None of them are as life threatening as hypothermia. Frostnip is that transient pain on the tips of the fingers when your fingers have gotten too cold. Trenchfoot is a cold water immersion injury where your wet feet have suffered too much cold. Chillblains are itchy sores usually on the hands from too much exposure to cold and damp and tend to heal poorly.

Frostbite is the other significant cold injury. There is actual tissue injury and death with blistering. The tissue turns red, dark, and then black. The damage, however, is often less than it appears. The take home message for the outdoors adventurer is that treatment is to warm the extremity and take every precaution to avoid refreezing. If you cannot guarantee that the injury will not refreeze, please leave it alone until you can. Protect the frozen part from shear or pressure injuries. Do not rub with snow. Keep as dry as possible.

Heat related injuries can also be life threatening. The two types that cause the most concern are heat exhaustion and heat stroke.

Heat exhaustion is excessive body heat that builds up by prolonged physical activities. It is accompanied by excessive sweating and exhaustion. You can notice a change in mental status, such as irritability or even euphoria. Ice packs and moist towels in addition to oral rehydration and rest are often enough treatment.

Heat stroke is a medical emergency! There is alteration of the mental status (confusion) and a body temperature of greater than 41°C (106°F). It is associated with dehydration and dry skin and is often accompanied with multiple organ failure. Risks include obesity, poor physical conditioning (recognize the theme), and dehydration. Treatment involves immediate cooling and is best accomplished by immersion in a cool water/ice bath, hospitalization, and IV fluids. Anytime that you see a confused warm person, think of this potentially life threatening condition

Prevention of weather related injuries is easy unless you get caught unprepared. Dress appropriately in layers that you can add and remove. Wear moisture wicking clothes like polyester for cold conditions and cotton for warmer conditions. Keep well hydrated, and try to avoid exhaustion.

Weather related injuries are only part of the many injuries that can occur while experiencing your outdoor adventure as a WILDERNESS HUNTER. The next chapters will deal with others and their treatment.

Chapter Seven

- - - - - - - - - - - - - - - - - -

▪ Other hunting injuries... interesting and potentially fatal

- - - - - - - - - - - - - - - - - -

He was a Pennsylvania State policeman. As an excellent hunter, he was looking forward to the first day of archery hunting season. As he approached his tree stand, he realized that he was tired but those extra shifts that he had worked to get this vacation time were well worth it. He carefully climbed into the stand and buckled himself in. He tried to fight off the sleep, but he ultimately succumbed to it. When the rescue team found him, the evidence suggested that he had fallen out of the tree stand and his restraint had suffocated him.

Other than firearms accidents, which we will not discuss here, the most troubling and potentially preventable hunting injury is the tree stand injury. Almost everyone who has used a tree stand has had an "accident." Fortunately most of them are of little or no consequences. And most occur during the climb into and out of the stand.

Why are tree stand injuries included with Wilderness Hunting? It is because you may be alone with a life threatening injury and you may need to call upon your skills as a WILDERNESS HUNTER.

I do not know what it is about tree stands that tend to

make us careless. We know that they are great tools that give us an unprecedented advantage in our sport. It is like being in an open-air theatre, enjoying the many sights and sounds of nature. That relaxing atmosphere belies the danger of the situation. You need to maintain eternal vigilance when you are in the stand.

You can ask any tree stand hunter and they will tell you that tree stand safety involves the proper selection of the tree, the proper stand and harness, and good entry, climb, and exit techniques. If that is so well understood, why are there so many accidents?

I think that some of it relates to the fact that we are anxious to get on stand. We have made a cautious sniper's approach to the stand, which took time, and we know that the sooner we get on stand the less likely it is that our quarry will locate us.

Fatigue, sleep, and sometimes alcohol are often involved in tree stand injuries. Sometimes it is the stand itself, having been poorly constructed or neglected. Some hunters feel that a tree stand is the ideal place to take a nap. Wrong! Restraints and chains fail or there are unexpected wind gusts. Climbing stands have been known to slip.

Permanent tree stands that are neglected from year to year are a cause for concern. You need to maintain them regularly. Shooting rails are strongly encouraged, as they may add an extra margin of safety. If you use a climbing stand, you really should practice at home where you can better control the circumstance. Most importantly, you need to practice and master the technique of using a safety-climbing belt any time that you use a climber. This is not easy to learn! It is my personal opinion that ladder stands may have an edge on safety over climbing stands, but I do not know of any data that would support my conclusion.

Knife wounds are the most common hunting injuries that our local emergency rooms see during hunting season. I suppose that you could add lacerations from broad head arrows to this equation. Almost all of the knife wounds occur while skinning or dressing the animal. Some occur during processing.

There is a science to using a knife. There are advocates that feel a four-inch blade is the optimal size to skin and dress an animal. If you are going to use a folding knife, it must absolutely have a lock back feature. Please, only one person at a time while dressing the animal. Keep the knife sharp. Dull knives cause injuries because of the excessive force that it takes to cut through tissue. There are plenty of lightweight inexpensive sharpeners out there that you should carry with you. Do not forget to have a brightly colored marking on your knife so that you can see where you have laid it so that you do not cut yourself when trying to retrieve it. You must have a good sheath for a straight knife.

Many injuries that occur are secondary to "natural causes." This does not make them any less dangerous, but they are harder to control.

Everyone worries about snakebites, especially in the rattlesnake-infested area in Pennsylvania where I hunt. But beestings are far more dangerous than rattlesnake bites because they are far more common and cause immediate swelling of the airways and sudden circulatory collapse. This is called an anaphylactic reaction and is surprisingly common.

There are four types of bees, and stings from all types can be lethal. Most hunters know that they are allergic to beestings, but sometimes these reactions can occur unexpectedly. Even if you have not had a serious reaction to the sting of a particular bee, there is no guarantee that the next sting from that same type of bee will not cause a life threatening anaphylactic reaction. There is emergency treatment available that you can carry with you available by prescription, called an EPI pen. Besides carrying an EPI pen with you during warm weather, the sensitive hunter should seriously consider allergy desensitization program if they had a history of a serious reaction.

How important is it that you carry an EPI pen? Back in the "old days" of internal medicine, if you did not carry epinephrine with you to your internal medicine certification exam, it was grounds for failing your exam. In warmer weather I carry an EPI pen with me not only for my use but in case another hunter or my guide would need it. (You have to protect those guides!)

Sprains/strains/fractures are about as predictable as rain in the spring in Pennsylvania. It is often not important to know the differences because they all can hurt the same. It is far more important that you know how to treat, immobilize, and transport the hunter that has one. For the initial phase, Rest, Ice, Compression, and Elevation (RICE) of the injured part may help. This is usually followed by immobilization as necessary. Obvious fractures need to be splinted, preferably in an "anatomical position" to insure adequate blood flow.

The anatomical position is the position that a "normal extremity" would have at rest.

Please, please, please assume that every hunter that has fallen, especially from a height or has lost consciousness, has sustained a neck injury! Assume this even if they are not complaining of neck pain because if they have another injury that is causing severe pain (a distracting injury), they may not feel the pain right away. You have to immobilize the neck any way that you can until proper help arrives. A thick blanket or an extra jacket wrapped around the neck may provide a minimum of support. It is your job to make sure that the hunter's head does not move from side to side or back to front during transport.

Ideally, if the injury involves an extremity, the injured part should be evaluated by a health professional prior to use. In some situations, however, such as extreme hunting remote from medical evacuation, exceptions may have to be made. In these situations, if the hunter is able to use the injured part (extremity injuries only) without too much pain and self-ambulation is the only expedient way to evacuate, "You got to do what you got to do." Survival takes precedent to injury management.

There are many more injuries that can occur. As a WILDERNESS HUNTER, I highly recommend that you take a first aid course prior to any potentially extreme or extreme hunting situation. If you still do not feel comfortable with your knowledge, there are numerous first aid manuals that are compact and can take you through injury management step by step. However, remember Murphy's Law: most likely when you need the manual it will not be available to you. Thus, it is important that you understand at least the basics.

Suggestions for other injuries:

Lightning strikes

If the person appears dead and does not have a pulse, start CPR and give a "sternal thump" (pounding the breastbone sharply with a closed fist). This may generate enough electric current to restart their heart. NOT MANY HEALTH CARE SPECIALISTS RECOMMEND THIS! And there are not any controlled studies that I know of. But if a defibrillator is not immediately available on your wilderness trek, it cannot hurt because this is a LAST DITCH DESPERATE MEASURE!

Snake bites

"Less is more" is probably the best philosophy. Up to 40% of rattlesnake bites are "dry" and do not result in a significant envenomation. You will probably know quickly if a significant envenomation has occurred because of pain and swelling. Regardless, immobilize the extremity and have the victim drink lots of fluids. The vast majority of techniques described in books to get rid of venom have little use in the field. Prompt evacuation is the best treatment. You almost certainly will have enough time to do so before the patient decompensates.

Burns

Remove from heat source. Cover the burn with an occlusive dressing to prevent infection and hypothermia.

Corneal abrasions and foreign bodies in the eye

Carry a little bottle of contact lens solution to irrigate the eye. Patch eye lightly to reduce sunlight and to protect the eye. Seek medical attention as quickly as possible.

Blisters

The best treatment is prevention. You can cover with moleskin and protect from additional injury. It is best not to drain.

There are many more possible injuries and we will discuss some of the first aid tricks in the next chapter.

Chapter Eight

- **First aid...preparation is an important part of hunting**

As we have mentioned in the last chapter, one of the most important things that you can do is to take a first aid course and carry a small handbook of first aid. As a WILDERNESS HUNTER you have an ethical obligation to know basic first aid in order to help yourself and fellow hunters. Besides, getting yourself or your fellow hunter back on their feet may save your hunt.

Remember your ABC's

In addition to a first aid course, I highly recommend that you take a CPR class offered in many locations by Red Cross and local ambulance services and hospitals. I cannot imagine anyone going on an extended trip with a hunting buddy that would not take the time to learn these critical skills. You are an outdoor adventurer, a hunter! You have to know these skills. As a WILDERNESS HUNTER you must be more knowledgeable than most because you will be in harm's way more often. Learn how to use an AED (Automatic External Defibrillator). A significant part of your time may be traveling where an AED is immediately available.

Studies have shown that the most life saving measure for cardiac arrest is early defibrillation. Unless you are on a plane or in an airport, you will not have access to an electronic defibrillator. Do the best that you can. Survival in the field with prolonged CPR is dismal. It doesn't mean that you shouldn't try. If the person does not respond in the first 5-10 minutes, it is highly unlikely that they will survive. Fortunately, hunting has fewer than predicted episodes of cardiac arrest.

When someone collapses or is unresponsive and an AED is not available, you must remember Airway, Breathing, Circulation (Blue is bad, pink is good, air moves in and out, blood goes round and round!). Making sure that the person's airway is clear is the most important step. The airway is the mouth and the breathing tube. But remember, if there is any chance of a neck injury you have to protect the neck while you are doing this. You have to make sure that they are moving air in and out, and if they are not, you must do so for them with whatever means you have.

Stop all bleeding by whatever means you have. Direct pressure on the wound is the most effective method, even on deep wounds. Use the cleanest dressing that you have, even if it is not sterile. You seldom need a tourniquet, but if the bleeding from an extremity will not stop using by using as much direct pressure as you can give, it may be lifesaving.

Clean all open wounds with the cleanest water that you have. If the wound is obviously contaminated with dirt, rinse it thoroughly with water to try to get all of the visible dirt out. If the only thing you have is tap water, fine. Try to find some way to use pressure to irrigate the wound. If you can boil and cool water, that is even better. Then apply a clean dressing.

Remember to keep the victim warm. This is one of
the most overlooked problems in first aid in the field.
Hypothermia (low body temperature) complicates
all treatment and decreases the victim's likelihood of
surviving.

First aid kits...you really should consider them
emergency medical kits

I plead guilty! It's my training in emergency medicine
that makes me think that first aid kits should be
considered emergency medical kits. I believe this
because on potential extreme hunts or extreme hunts,
you will be doing far more than first aid, especially if
medical evacuation is problematic. But for now we still
call them first aid kits.

You have to purchase or build a first aid kit based upon
the type of hunting that you are doing. There are
many high quality first aid kits on the market as I have
mentioned before. You do not have to be too particular
if you are on a casual hunt where the car is nearby
(please remember to carry your EPI pen with you in
warm weather). On those types of hunts, you can have
a first aid kit that has everything including the kitchen
sink.

It gets to be more of a problem as your hunting becomes
more extreme. As I have mentioned before, there is an
inverse relationship between the size of your first aid kit
and the difficulty of your hunting. This is why the more

extreme the hunt, the more important it is for you to design your own first aid kit.

Unlike most health care professionals, I do not recommend a stand alone first aid kit for the potentially extreme and the extreme hunting situations. The following statement is so important that if this is the only thing that you learn form this book, it will have been well worth the price of the book!

EACH WILDERNESS HUNTER SHOULD MAKE EVERY EFFORT POSSIBLE TO COMBINE AN EMERGENCY MEDICAL KIT WITH A SURVIVAL KIT TO MAKE ONE NEAT SMALL PACKAGE OR PACKAGES JUST ADEQUATELY SUITED TO THAT TYPE OF HUNT...AND THAT IT WILL BE CARRIED ALMOST UNNOTICED BY THE HUNTER!

I cannot over emphasize the importance of being able to carry your emergency/survival kit by you unnoticed. If it is an extra burden, you will not carry it.

We talked about survival equipment in a previous chapter. It only makes sense to combine it with your emergency medical kit (first aid kit). You can carry it in a game pouch or distribute in several pockets. I like the idea of a survival belt pack. Figure out something that will suit you and your hunting. But whatever you choose, the kit has to be light and unobtrusive. There also is one more challenge...

The personal medical kit

The older the hunter, the more likely he or she will have medical problems. We will talk about this in a later chapter. Regardless of how old you are, you are going to need special medications that suit your individual needs. In my case I also carry common medications for fellow hunters and the guide. The personal medical kit should be considered an expansion of the basic first aid kit. The same rules apply as above.

It takes a little finesse to design your own personal medical kit. I suggest that you recruit your personal physician to help you design this kit. The more extreme the hunt, the more the components of the kit have to be capable of treating more than one condition, because you cannot take everything with you.

This kit includes your personal medications and over the counter medications (OTCs), which are not in your first aid kit. It should include an antibiotic capable of treating traveler's diarrhea, skin infections, urinary track infections, and respiratory infections. A medication like ciprofloxacin or doxycycline may be a good choice. A medication for pain is a must (e.g., Lorcet). The more extreme the hunt, the more important this is because you may have to walk a long distance in considerable pain. An eye ointment is necessary for corneal abrasions and conjunctivitis and can be used as wound ointments (e.g., Ocuflox). Rounding out the top medication choices are topical steroid/antifungal creams (e.g., Lotrisone), burn cream (e.g., Silvadine) and a migraine medication (e.g., Imitrex). It amazes me how many people have migraine headaches, which are brought on by lack of sleep, dehydration, altitude, and lack of caffeine. It also amazes me how many people have altitude induced headaches, some of which are helped by migraine medications.

Occasionally I will throw in some acupuncture needles into my kit. For those that know how to use them, they can be helpful for extremity injuries such as ankle sprains and bruises on prolonged hunts where resting and medical treatment is otherwise not an option. Traumeel is an ointment that can help quickly reduce pain and swelling.

I apologize for not covering other first aid scenarios in this book, but as a WILDERNESS HUNTER you will learn them in your first aid course. One other thing, though. You should always give consideration to carry some source of hot fluids and some source of fast acting sugar. You do this not for yourself but for some lost hunter you may come upon whom may be dehydrated or hypoglycemic.

We will now move on to special conditions that deserve our vigilance.

Chapter Nine

- **Altitude sickness...why it deserves its own chapter**

When I first started writing this book, I was only going to mention altitude injuries casually. Since that time, I have discovered that there are many WILDERNESS HUNTERS and outdoors adventurers that suffer from this, far more than I originally thought. For this reason and since the "dream hunt of a lifetime" for many hunters is a mountain hunt, I decided to give this topic the attention that it deserves.

If there is one medical condition that can ruin an otherwise good hunt for the WILDERNESS HUNTER, it has to be altitude illnesses. The sad thing is that for many ruined hunts, this is totally preventable. And prevention is easy, unless you are going on an ultra high altitude hunt in Asia or elsewhere.

Altitude related illness usually starts occurring at altitudes above 8,000 feet MSL. Headache is the most common symptom. If left unrecognized and untreated, the symptoms can progress to include fluid in the lungs and brain, conditions called high altitude pulmonary edema (HAPE) and high altitude cerebral edema (HACE). The latter two conditions can be life-threatening events. With HAPE, cough and difficulty breathing can become progressive without treatment.

With HACE, the most serious of them all, the brain starts to swell and confusion becomes prevalent. This presents a problem because the hunter can become uncooperative with the treatment of choice. In this case, descent to a lower altitude.

Altitude illness can often involve younger persons rather than older persons. This may be the one exception to the rule that younger individuals are usually able to adapt to changing environments quicker than older individuals. Other risk factors for altitude illness include poor physical conditioning, dehydration, lack of sleep, alcohol use, and the lack of time to accommodate to altitude.

There are legions of books about preventing altitude illness. The prevention, however, is relatively easy. Almost all experts in this topic recommend the use of acetazolamide (Diamox), a type of diuretic (fluid pill) that can and should be prescribed for you by your personal physician. Treatment is usually begun several days before the trip and continues for a short period of time thereafter. The judicious and proper use of this medication can prevent the vast majority of altitude related illnesses, but it is not guaranteed. However, it does have a side effect. You may have to get out of that warm sleeping bag in the middle of the night to urinate, because that is what the diuretic is supposed to do! That side effect may be minimal at the newly recommended lower dosage for acetazolamide.

There is a recent flurry of discussion that some of the supplements can help prevent or treat altitude illness. Ginkgo biloba is one of them but is less effective than Diamox. Why risk the chance of ruining your dream hunt and that of others by not taking the best preventive treatment. And if any of you have been on a hunt or other outdoor excursion where a member has suffered one of the more severe forms of altitude illness, you know what I am talking about. It ruins everyone's hunt.

Not every WILDERNESS HUNTER needs Diamox. But on your first trip to altitude, I think that you should give it a try if your personal physician agrees. Once you have experienced altitude for prolonged periods of time on multiple trips, you begin to appreciate how susceptible you are. Do not take a chance, however, if medical help and descent to a lower altitude is not an option.

There are many other things that you can do to prevent altitude illness. Here is a list of my favorites:

- ☑ Avoid camping at altitudes over 9,000 feet MSL

- ☑ Do not ascend more than 1,500 feet a day

- ☑ Drink plenty of water to avoid dehydration

- ☑ Make sure that you have been reasonably decaffeinated

- ☑ Avoid the use of alcohol

- ☑ Moderate your activities for the first several days

- ☑ Take extra time to become adapted

- ☑ Train low, sleep high

☑ Try to get plenty of rest

☑ Be in the best physical condition that you can be in

Three of these deserve additional discussion. There may be a role for altitude training to prevent high altitude illness. The problem is that you quickly lose your adaptation to high altitude. A number that is often quoted is 10 days. This means that if you go to the mountains for training and return home before your hunt, you will lose your adaptation to altitude within 10 days. Likewise, it takes time to adapt to altitude. This may occur more quickly than 10 days, but not necessarily. The standard recommendation that you should go to your hunt site several days before your trip to accommodate is always good advice, but most of us do not have that extra time and it may not be time enough or high enough for us to fully adapt.

I have recently been toying with the idea of using an altitude chamber to prepare for altitude hunts. These are portable rentable sleep chambers that the mountaineering community has been using for a while. This type of training is probably not necessary for most hunts in the lower forty eight, but for those individuals that are particularly susceptible to the effects of altitude and for those hunters who are going to Asia for extremely high altitude hunts, it only makes sense. This is an application of the principle of altitude training, where you should "sleep high and train low." And as always, consult your personal physician before using such a device.

Caffeine is ubiquitous in our diet and many of us are dependent upon it. In some individuals, caffeine makes their headaches better, and in others, it makes their headache worse. But caffeine withdrawal can cause severe headaches. Caffeine can also both cause and prevent migraine headaches. In addition, if you are prone to migraines, all of the stresses of hunting can aggravate migraines. These include fatigue, physical exhaustion, foods high in preservatives (e.g., jerky, lunchmeats, pickles, pepperoni sticks), and dehydration. Typically you end up with a severe headache at day 3-4 of the hunt. The problem lies in trying to figure out whether this is altitude illness or migraine headache.

The best advice I can give you is to relatively decaffeinate yourself before an extreme hunt at altitude. Cut yourself down to the barest minimum. For instance, cutback to 1-2 cups of caffeinated beverages daily before you go to altitude. And if you are caffeine dependent, bring some instant coffee or tea with you. Your guide may not have any, and that is a bad thing. Trust me!

We could go on for hours about altitude illnesses, but now it is time to move on to another huge challenge for the WILDERNESS HUNTER...how to get yourself fueled for the adventure!

Chapter Ten

- **Food, water, and supplements...your fuel to get you to your destination**

With casual hunts, your food and water options are easy. You will have easy access to whatever you want. The same can be said for potentially extreme hunts...until they become extreme! The extreme hunt is where you have to pack in your own food is an entirely different matter.

Regardless of the type of hunting that you are doing, you should always carry some type of calorie dense of packaged food/drink. You never know when you are going to run across a hunter with low blood sugar or when your outing becomes longer than it was planned to be. If at all possible during cold weather, you should also carry a small thermos filled with hot chocolate or some other warm beverage that sweeteners can be added to. Even on backpack sheep hunts, I often carry a pint-sized thermos because there are some things like a warm cup of coffee or hot chocolate that just cannot be forsaken!

There are those that say alcohol and hunting do not mix. For the most part, I agree. But when you are done for the day, alcohol in moderation is probably all right. One back pack sheep hunter that I know who has been on 22 different sheep hunts told me that he carries a small flask of scotch whiskey with him "just to make some sense out of the whole ordeal!"

When you are talking about extreme hunts, you are talking about dehydrated or freeze dried foods. There are a lot of high quality freeze-dried foods. MREs (Meals Ready to Eat) tend to be a little heavy on backpack hunts but may be perfectly fine if they can be transported by some other means. Couscous is a favorite. It weighs little and fills your stomach. Lots of hunters like the flavor packs from Ramen noodle soup. They can jazz about anything up, including sheep ribs! Power Bars, trail mix, jerky, and chocolate bars keep you going. Most mountaineers just keep munching all day. Plan on losing about a pound a day of body weight on the vigorous hunt. Garth Carter of The Huntin' Fool likes Ore Ida instant potatoes to add to the Mountain House meals.

On the top of the list for calories per weight, it is hard to beat cashews. Although the dehydrated meals that are found in camping stores tend to be pricey, they are worth every penny. But for the other food items mentioned, they are quite reasonably priced and readily available at discount stores like Walmart. If your trek is going to be markedly prolonged, take some protein powder that you can add to just about anything. It may be just the ticket for you to save your muscle strength.

Discussion about vitamins and supplements always raises heated arguments, much like the discussion of what is the best caliber of gun to take on an elk hunt. In my experience, most of the readily available commercial multivitamins with 1,000 units of Vitamin D are excellent bargains and well worth the investment. Although it has been beaten up by the cardiologists, there have been convincing arguments that Vitamin E can prevent the delayed onset of muscle soreness. Vitamin C in a reasonable dosage, say 1,000 milligrams daily, seems to help many avoid colds and respiratory problems. The evidence with other vitamins is less convincing, but if you are convinced that they help you, go for it.

The evidence with the supplements is weaker. Other than the fact that glucosamine with chondroitin (e.g., Joint Support, Osteo Bi Flex) seems to help about 40% of individuals, including me, few of the other supplements show consistent benefit. When patients ask me whether a particular supplement will help them, I tell them that it has a 10% chance, but if you are in that 10%, good for you! But 90% of the time you are wasting your money (It is your money though).

With regards to supplements, there may be two other exceptions. We have already talked about Ginkgo biloba and its ability to prevent and treat mountain sickness. Recently Co Q 10 in 100 milligram dosages has been found useful to prevent soreness from certain lipid lowering medications and to improve your stamina. Recent evidence suggests that quercetin supplementation also improves stamina.

When you are going on an extreme hunt, you have to have some reserve that you can fall back on. I lost a good friend many years ago because he canoed rough water while recovering from a weakened state due to a dental condition. He just was not strong enough and did not have the reserve to fight the hypothermia from cold water. Cold weather is no time to go on a calorie-restricted diet. Fats are a necessary source of energy to stay warm. In your preparation for one of the extreme hunts, you should not let yourself get in a calorie-depleted state. A little "jiggle" is OK!

Your water needs are best served by a filter or chemical treatment if the purity of the water is questionable. Purification tablets weigh next to nothing if taken out of the jar and put into a dark small plastic container. If you object to the taste of iodinated water, add a little ascorbic acid (vitamin C) to it. It will blunt the taste. Experiment with this at home to determine the correct dosage.

If it is an emergency situation and you have no option, drink the cleanest water that you can find. We physicians can always treat you later. Try to always carry an extra water bottle with you. You will drink more water if it has some flavor like those little packaged flavor straws of green tea.

There are many high quality filtering water devices, ozone purifiers, and ultraviolet units. Discussion of these units is like trying to shoot a moving target. Each year the equipment keeps getting better and better. Backpacker magazine often has discussions about this. Check with your local mountaineering store for up to date equipment.

One of the lightest and most indestructible water bottles is the 20 oz size of plastic soda bottles. I have seen them survive hundreds of feet drops. Try to carry an extra one filled with water if you do not have access to a ready source. The only problem is that they do not have a wide mouth. But as a spare, they cannot be beat!

Now that we have you fed and watered it is time to talk about the next topic, clothing and footwear for the WILDERNESS HUNTER.

Chapter Eleven

- -

- **Clothing and footwear... your only
   defense against the weather**

- -

If there is any area that the WILDERNESS HUNTER
should concentrate on in preparing for any type of hunt,
it would be clothing and footwear. It is your only defense
against the often unpredictable weather.

Fortunately, the choices of outdoor clothing keep
getting better and better. What weighed pounds
years ago now weigh ounces. The new synthetics wick
moisture and some are even impregnated with chemicals
that keep you from smelling too bad late into your hunt.
There is wind stopping material and lightweight rain
gear.

For unadulterated rain protection, there is nothing
better than rubber or nylon such as the rain suits like
Helly Hansen or Peter Storm. Designed for fisherman,
these suits tend to be too heavy for general hunting
applications other than casual hunting. The exception
might be materials like Impertech offered by Helly
Hansen.

Goretex works well but will eventually get wet. I like
backpacker's suits like Red Ledge Thunderlight or if I
need to go lighter, Ultralight Packable rain gear from
Cabela's, which tends to be more fragile but is easy

to repair with, you guessed it, duct tape. My personal choice is to wear simple Goretex jeans, which eventually will leak, and to have an ultralight suit as backup. Sitka makes good rain gear also.

If you are not a backpacker, any of the heavier insulated rain suits may fit the bill. I suggest that you get several catalogs from the major sporting goods chains and start to study the different types of rain wear. Ask your outfitter or other hunters what works for them. One thing is sure, however. By the time you are done, you will have several different types of rain gear, each perfectly suited to different situations. As always, buy quality.

I grew up with Woolrich clothing. I could not imagine today, however, not wearing clothing that I can layer. When I am hunting a certain stand that involves an hour plus walk in the dark, up and down several hills, I will wear a cotton sweatshirt, which will absorb the sweat. When I get close to my destination, I will remove this, put it in a plastic garbage bag, and then put on my polyester base, polyester shirt, fleece with or without windstopper, and my jacket. It works well for me but maybe not for you. My brother-in-law wears cotton long underwear and a complete one-piece suit. He can get away with that because he hardly sweats. He can stay outdoors all day! He just carries a slip on rain suit.

When you are on an extreme hunt like a backpack hunt, however, you must learn the layering technique. This is because you cannot carry any extra weight. You are participating in that quintessential sheep hunter's struggle of weight versus performance. With the new material it is amazing that, if you choose to do it, you can do a 10-day backpack sheep hunt with only one change of clothes!

Most synthetics dry quickly. Often all that you have to do is to wear them after it quits raining or snowing and your body heat will dry them. The same cannot be said for wool or cotton. Although cotton is excellent for hot and humid conditions, its use is highly discouraged in cold damp environments. Wool will keep you warm, but it is heavy and gets heavier when wet. It may be unbeatable, however, for casual hunts. There is a place for a good wool sweater and cap for the backpacker if there is a chance you may get wet, because unlike most material, wool will keep you relatively warm even if it gets wet. You just will have to keep your woolen garments to a minimum, however.

When you choose your clothing, you might want to choose an insulating material that performs even when it is wet. Some of the synthetics like Primaloft will do so, whereas down will not. The beauty of down, however, is that it is exceptionally light for its ability to insulate. Sometimes you can have the best of both worlds by having down incorporated into a waterproof material, like some of the high-end sleeping bags or vests. I have heard of treated down that is impervious to moisture, although I haven't seen it yet. I always carry a down vest but I take exceptional care that it does not get wet, and I always have a backup layering plan. My next investment will be a Primaloft vest.

The same rules for clothing apply to sleeping bags. For most wilderness hunts, a sleeping bag like the Cat's Meow should be adequate. I use a Cabela's down Boundary Waters bag. You can extend the temperature range of the bag by using a bag liner or by wearing your insulated clothes to bed. Sleeping bag technology improves daily and there are an infinite number of other choices available.

A sleeping pad is essential. Try not to skimp on this. The Z-pads should be a minimum. Campmor sell the Thermarest Pro-lite, which has received accolades. Just remember, anything that inflates may be punctured on your trip. Plan for this.

Boots demand the utmost of attention. Poorly fitting or inferior quality boots have ruined more wilderness adventures than anything else. You will need more than one pair depending on the types of hunts that you do. Here in Pennsylvania, where most hunting is casual or potentially extreme, you can often get by with a single pair of boots. Many hunters that I know are gravitating to slip on rubber boots like Muck boots because they are scent free, comfortable in most conditions, and waterproof and light. Last year I did a mountain goat hunt with a guide that wore a pair similar to this. Bird hunters will not be very happy with them because there is too much walking in warmer weather, and soft leather is the ticket. Most of us get by with a pair of Goretex insulated boots, with or without scent blocker. When the weather gets extremely cold, you must go to packs and I think that if you are doing a lot of stand hunting, over boots are a great idea, much like layering for your clothes.

When you get to the extreme mountain hunts, however, all bets are off. You absolutely must get your boots right...right for you and right for conditions. When I first got into this type of hunting, I spent more time

choosing boots than any other part of my gear. They
have to be rugged, waterproof, relatively light, and
provide good ankle support. At the suggestion of my
first outfitter, I purchased a pair of Alaskan Meindl
boots through Cabela's. These boots, in addition to
the Canadian Hunter model, have been the standard
fare for many sheep hunters. Because I had recently
fractured my ankle, I needed all of the support that I
could have, and these boots gave it. They were absolutely
the right choice for this hunt, and I am on my third pair.

For my second sheep hunt in Montana, however, I
discovered a particularly nasty brown rock in Unit 501
that turns slick with moisture. The hard Vibram soles
of the Meindl's were completely useless. My guide had
a much more flexible pair of Sherpa Mountaineering
boots that got much better traction and I suffered dearly
trying to keep up with him. The forward somersault with
my pack and gun while losing my footing in a rockslide
did not help either. I got a pair of Kennetreks with softer
soles and presumably better grip. I cannot wait to try
them out!

And so it is with mountain boots…you are always looking
for a better pair. Whatever you do, make sure that before
you go on that hunt that you have broken the boots in
and "tweaked them" as I have described in an earlier
chapter. Some boots come nearly broken in while others
will require work.

One last piece of clothing that you must give careful
attention to is your head gear. Estimates vary on the
amount of body heat that you lose through your head
from 20- 40%. I wear a Goretex ball cap in all weather.
When it is cold, I put a fleece over cap with ear flaps. I

believe that you lose as much heat through your neck and face as you do through your scalp. That is why a fleece balaclava in extremely cold conditions will give you an edge. You can always use the hood of that ultra light rain jacket that you carry as additional wind protection.

For most of us the super sporting goods stores and the large discount stores will provide us with everything that we need. One sheep outfitter told me that everyone shows up like they stepped out of a Cabela's catalog. There are, however, many other places that you should check out such as backpacker, camping, and mountaineering stores.

Always buy quality. It never ceases to amaze me that I am still wearing an original pair of polypropelene long underwear that I bought 17 years ago and that they still are in great shape!

Make sure that your clothing has enough pockets to carry your essentials and make sure that you have some fluorescent orange to meet the hunting requirements and to use for signaling. One other item of gear that you might want to consider is your own personal one man tent with a vestibule. If you are the type of person who snores or who cannot put up with other people snoring or getting jammed in the face by the guide's elbow or worse, this option may appeal to you. Yes, it is extra weight, but if you have the excess capacity in your pack, it is well worth considering a 2-pound tent. One again, this is personal choice but you may want to discuss this with your guide and outfitter.

There is so much more to talk about: mountaineering

equipment, backpacks, gun carriers, etc. But it is time to move on to travel medicine for the WILDERNESS HUNTER.

Chapter Twelve

———————————————————————

- **Travel medicine for the international wilderness hunter and adventurer... medical advice for strange places**

———————————————————————

It never ceases to amaze me the number of travelers that number of foreign business travelers from my small county. As the World Grand Slam of wild sheep and Capra wild goat slams gain in prestige for the mountain hunters, more and more hunters are traveling to clandestine destinations in Asia, Africa, South America, and Australia/New Zealand. An African hunt may cost less than a quality elk or mule deer hunt. On any given excursion to a foreign country, it is estimated that 10% of the participants will require some health care.

Travel medicine has recently caught on in the U.S. because there are many older adventurers traveling today. This creates unique problems. I am really excited about a new organization called Expedition Medicine, which had its first national conference last year. This organization is dedicated to the safety, health, and welfare of the participants in expeditions, often to quite remote places.

Travel medicine is mostly about preparation. You have to be prepared for any emergency because in some

remote locations the access to quality health care just
is not there. This is one time when a high quality first
aid manual may be important to you if you do not have
health training. You may be reading that manual by
candlelight and directing healthcare for yourself or a
fellow hunter or even a guide!

Most international hunters are in reasonable shape,
but they tend to be older and have at least one or two
medical problems. Because of the nature of hunting,
you can almost be guaranteed that you will not have
access to quality health care, unlike the tourists to trendy
locations. The following are some simple suggestions.

First of all, most overseas accidents and injuries are
motor vehicle related. Robert Rodale, the founder of
Prevention magazine, was killed while crossing a street
in South America. Vehicular maintenance is on an as
needed basis in many countries. Driver safety may be
non-existent. Be extra cautious when crossing the street
or choosing the vehicles and drivers that transport you
and your goods.

Secondly, most illnesses that occur while traveling are
routine: common colds, bronchitis, flu, and traveler's
diarrhea. You must prepare for these ahead of time
and have the necessary treatment available with you.
You need to be updated with your normal vaccines like
tetanus shots, flu shots, and pneumonia vaccines as age
appropriate.

As we discussed earlier, many sheep hunters to Asia
say the most important safety item that they have is a
satellite cell phone. You cannot depend on local guides
to have reliable means of communication. Your life

may depend upon this especially if you need a higher level of emergency care such as an emergency medical evacuation.

Next is emergency medical evacuation insurance. Choose a reputable agency. Find out ahead of time just what they will cover. The language that they may use may not mean what you think it means. They may take you to the nearest facility rather than the facility of your choice. You have to spend extra time researching this. You may be required to have emergency surgery locally. Generally speaking, the emergency surgery is not usually the problem. It is the tainted blood products and the post op care that are life threatening. Be sure that you have a choice of where to go for these critical issues.

A cardinal rule for all travelers is to keep your immune system primed. You best do this by a proper diet, enough rest, avoiding tobacco and alcohol to excess, and by taking supplemental vitamins. Please do not suddenly stop the vitamin program that you have been taking at home. You will end up with a relative vitamin deficiency and almost surely some sort of upper respiratory infection.

You need to learn about and practice proper food and water handling. Most American types of hotels have water purification and good food hygiene. Most others do not. Do not eat any fruits that you cannot peel or any uncooked vegetables, especially fresh salads. One item that most travelers forget about is the ice that is put into drinks. It may come from contaminated sources.

If you take prescription medications, you must take some precautions. Keep your medication in two separate locations. For instance carry half of your daily supply of prescriptions with you at all times and the other half in your luggage. That way if you get separated from your luggage you will have a chance to replenish them. Make sure that your medical kit has clearly marked labels. Border agents like labels. You may need a letter from your physician on "official letterhead" outlining your health problems and the medication that you are taking for them. Make sure that your physician labels the medicine by their generic names because the trade name may not be recognizable to a foreign health care provider. Maybe if you are especially nice to your personal physician, he or she may also help you put together an emergency medical kit.

As always, please inform your guide and your fellow hunters of your health conditions. The guide may not be of much help, but your fellow hunters may come to your rescue if you are suddenly incapacitated. Also, make sure that you take a small field guide of emergency medical care with you. I have had more than a few hunters tell me that they saved their hunting partner's hunt (and lives) by reading how to provide emergency care, sometimes even by candlelight!

Malaria is a problem in many remote areas. The first line of malaria prevention is to avoid the mosquito bite in the first place. This means DEET, long sleeved shirts, and an impregnated net if available. And of course, you always have to consider malaria prophylaxis. Some of the medicine prescribed for malaria has peculiar side effects, so your physician is going to have a discussion with you about the various options. There are resistant malarial strains that require special consideration.

A surprising number of health problems that occur overseas or in remote areas relate to dental issues. You need a good dental checkup prior to foreign travel of any duration. Ask your dentist if he or she can prepare an emergency dental kit for you if you lose a filling or chip a tooth.

Remember, HIV is endemic in many foreign countries. Please use discretion if you know what I mean! And flu epidemics are surprisingly common also.

Jet lag is a common problem for most travelers. Get plenty of rest, avoid excess alcohol, allow yourself time to accommodate, and ask your physician for additional recommendations.

Your entry into the world of travel medicine begins with your choice of health care providers. Many geographical regions have special immunization requirements that change periodically, often more than once yearly. The Centers for Disease Control and Prevention (CDC) has a website where you can research this. It is best to recruit a physician familiar with travel medicine to help you navigate through the process. This may be your personal physician; however, many areas have travel medicine clinics that can help you with your immunization and other travel needs. Travel Medicine physicians tend to be infectious disease specialists because most travel related disease of any importance seem to be related to infectious agents. Others are trained in tropical medicine or are emergency medicine physicians or primary care physicians with a special interest in travel medicine. If you need one, try to find a physician who is a member of the International Society of Travel Medicine.

Most primary care physicians, however, are capable of giving you solid travel advice if they have the time and interest to help you. If they do not, then you may have to find a travel medicine clinic. This clinic, however, is not a substitute for the personal relationship that you must have with your primary care physician, because he or she is going to have to help you organize your medical records, fill the necessary prescriptions, and help you with your medical travel kit.

If you are taking an extended trip, please get a good physical exam. Now is the time to get that hernia fixed, that troublesome gallbladder removed, those toenails fixed, or any other medical or surgical problem that you have been putting off. That includes a graded exercise stress test. Remember Murphy's Law...you will have problems. Don't take any chances.

Travel medicine does not stop when you return home. There are illnesses that you can contract in remote regions that only show up after you have returned home. Make an effort while you are hunting to learn about the local diseases so that you can give your physician a "heads up" upon your return, should you develop any problem.

Now for our final chapter...the older WILDERNESS HUNTER.

Chapter Thirteen

- **The older hunter...if this is not you now, it soon will be**

At the last Grand Slam convention, I met several hunters in their 80s who looked and acted at least twenty years younger. These are truly WILDERNESS HUNTERS! I have always believed that the most important key to longevity was an active lifestyle that includes at least moderate level of physical exercise. There is no doubt that exercise is the fountain of youth. If we could bottle it, it would be worth a fortune. There is nothing like mountain hunting to keep those longevity juices flowing!

As a group, we hunters are becoming an older. Often, it is only the older hunter that can afford some of the extreme hunting adventures that require wilderness training and preparation. Despite this there are many active WILDERNESS HUNTERS that are constantly proving that with regards to age and physical conditioning, "yesterday's sixty-five" can be "today's fifty." Whatever level of hunting that we choose, we need to keep our participation safe and not necessarily age appropriate, but level of fitness appropriate.

We older hunters have some unique handicaps but also some distinct advantages. The older adventurer/hunter is more likely to:

☑ Have co-morbid conditions (one or more potentially serious medical problems)

☑ Have some degree of arthritis

☑ Have more money

☑ May be less likely to suffer from altitude sickness

The challenge of the older adventurer is being felt everywhere in the travel industry and will require more participation by the healthcare community as the ever increasing number of outdoor adventurers suffer more injuries and illnesses while overseas. The following are some take home messages about these challenges.

Because the older hunter has more money, they can often afford the most clandestine activities. With these activities comes more risk, less availability to quality health care, and sometimes increased physical requirements. The high altitude sheep and goat hunts in Asia are a prime example of this. The older hunter has to be much more diligent in his or her planning and preparation for these adventures, especially with the ever present risk of altitude illness.

As you age you must learn how to retrain and rehabilitate yourself. You recover from injuries more slowly. It takes you longer to condition yourself. You loose your physical conditioning much faster. Because of arthritis you have to start shifting from high impact activities such as jogging to low impact activities such as biking. Fortunately for you the hunter, walking is a relatively low impact injury and is probably the safest form of exercise. You have to focus more on saving what you have rather than to "stretch the envelope."

Another important difference is that as you age, your diet will have a bigger impact on how well your training progresses and what your overall level of fitness will be. You must watch your calories more carefully because you will gain weight more rapidly. When you are young, you can eat just about anything without apparent ill effect. Not so for the older hunter! You have to watch your intake of fats because your cholesterol may be marginal, and you have to watch your salt intake a bit more carefully because of your borderline blood pressure. The older athlete is like an older fighter jet: less sensitive to its controls and high maintenance, but once they are tuned, they sure can fly!

Aging gracefully is hard work. But those of us that take the time to enjoy life will most likely be given more life to enjoy. There is no better way to accomplish this than as a WILDERNESS HUNTER in the physical challenge of the outdoor environment!

Conclusion

Sport hunting across the United States faces many challenges. It is up to each individual hunter to be the best ambassador that he or she can be. I strongly urge you to "step up" your hunting to become a WILDERNESS HUNTER if your personal physician agrees you can do so safely.

All of us outdoor adventurers need to encourage others to participate in the beauty and physical gifts that our natural environment gives us. This is especially true for the younger potential adventurer. Please mentor someone, especially a child, so that we can hand down this hunting legacy and our noble tradition can carry on.

Throughout this book I simplified complicated material and have given you what I consider the essence and basic principles of these topics. Many of these topics deserve their own books. If you are interested in further information about individual topics or a consultation, just drop me an email at:

msorg@outdoorsportsmedicine.com

You have chosen a noble sport. It is the perfect lifetime activity. Please use these principles to enjoy the sport safely and for many years. Become a WILDERNESS HUNTER!

About the Author

Dr. Sorg has been a hunter for forty-five years. For the past 15 years, he has hunted the Western states and Canada most recently including six backpack hunts. He is a 30-year veteran of primary care and emergency medicine and is board certified in Family Medicine, Emergency Medicine, certified in Sports Medicine, certified in acupuncture, and has a Master's Degree in Public Health. He is presently the medical director of his local hospital's cardiac rehabilitation department. He is an MD fellow of the Wilderness Medical Society. He and his wife a family physician, built, owned, and operated for 10 years the community's only complete health and recreational facility. This training and experience has given him a unique perspective about the health and fitness industry.

As a family physician first and foremost, Dr. Sorg has recognized that only information that is practical and easy to implement will stand the test of time and usefulness. Fitness fads come and go, but the basic principles are timeless. This book is meant to help you focus on the basics of what you need to know in the simplest possible way.